Mohammadreza Rast
Zahra Karimi Khoshhal

TOEFL Vocabulary Updates

Mohammadreza Rast
Zahra Karimi Khoshhal

TOEFL Vocabulary Updates

100 Vocabularies for TOEFL Test Candidates
Based on Merriam-webster Dictionary

Noor Publishing

Imprint

Any brand names and product names mentioned in this book are subject to trademark, brand or patent protection and are trademarks or registered trademarks of their respective holders. The use of brand names, product names, common names, trade names, product descriptions etc. even without a particular marking in this work is in no way to be construed to mean that such names may be regarded as unrestricted in respect of trademark and brand protection legislation and could thus be used by anyone.

Cover image: www.ingimage.com

Publisher:
Noor Publishing
is a trademark of
Dodo Books Indian Ocean Ltd. and OmniScriptum S.R.L publishing group

120 High Road, East Finchley, London, N2 9ED, United Kingdom
Str. Armeneasca 28/1, office 1, Chisinau MD-2012, Republic of Moldova, Europe
Printed at: see last page
ISBN: 978-620-7-47842-2

TOEFL Vocabulary Updates

100 Vocabularies for TOEFL Test Candidates
Based on Merriam-webster Dictionary

Compiled by :

Dr.Mohammadreza Rast

Zahra Karimi Khoshhal

Table of Contents

Preface

The upcoming book has been written to prepare language learners for the international TOEFL exam. The constant confusion of language learners in the field of finding a reliable and practical source for TOEFL vocabulary prompted me to compile a reliable and up-to-date reference of absolutely necessary and practical vocabulary based on the reality of these tests and not unrelated books to meet the needs of learners in All four main skills of listening, speaking, understanding and writing should be improved to a great extent.

Dr Mohammadreza Rast

January 2024

100 Vocabularies for TOEFL Test Candidates

accolade /ˈækəˌleɪd/ *noun*
plural **accolades**
[count]
: an award or an expression of praise

- There is no higher *accolade* at this school than an honorary degree.

— often plural

- She has been winning *accolades* [=she has been receiving praise] for her performances in small plays.
- The movie's special effects have drawn *accolades* from both fans and critics. [=have been praised by both fans and critics]

circumvent
/ˌsɚkəmˈvɛnt/
verb
circumvents; circumvented; circumventing
[+ object] *formal*
: to avoid being stopped by (something, such as a law or rule) : to get around (something) in a clever and sometimes dishonest way

— circumvention

/ˌsɚkəmˈvɛnʃən/ ***noun*** [noncount]

dearth
/ˈdɚθ/
noun
[singular] *formal*
: the state or condition of not having enough of something : LACK — + *of*

jargon
/ˈdʒɑɚgən/
noun
[noncount] *usually disapproving*
: the language used for a particular activity or by a particular group of people

[1] **labor** *(US)*
noun
or British **labour** /ˈleɪbɚ/
plural **labors**
1
a : physical or mental effort : WORK
[noncount][count]

◊ A **labor of love** is a task that you do for enjoyment rather than pay.

◊ When you **enjoy the fruits of your labor/labors,** you enjoy the things that you have gained by working.

b [noncount] **:** work for which someone is paid

2
[noncount]
a : workers considered as a group

— often used before another noun

b : the organizations or officials that represent groups of workers

3
: the process by which a woman gives birth to a baby
[noncount][singular]

4

Labour [singular] *British, politics* **:** the Labour Party of the United Kingdom or another part of the Commonwealth of Nations

² labor
/ˈleɪbɚ/
verb
(US) or British **labour**
labors; labored; laboring
[no object]
1
a : to do work

b : to work hard in order to achieve something

2
: to move or proceed with effort

3
: to repeat or stress something too much or too often

ludicrous
/ˈluːdəkrəs/
adjective
[more ludicrous; most ludicrous]
: very foolish : <u>RIDICULOUS</u>

— ludicrously

adverb

— ludicrousness

noun [noncount]

malice
/ˈmæləs/
noun
[noncount]
: a desire to cause harm to another person

mettle
/ˈmɛtl̩/
noun
[noncount]
: strength of spirit : ability to continue despite difficulties

on your mettle

chiefly British
: making an effort to do as well as possible

microcosm
/ˈmaɪkrəˌkɑːzəm/
noun
plural **microcosms**
[count]
: something (such as a place or an event) that is seen as a small version of something much larger

— compare MACROCOSM

in microcosm

: in a greatly reduced size or form

morose
/məˈroʊs/
adjective
[more morose; most morose]
1
of a person : very serious, unhappy, and quiet

2
: very sad or unhappy

— morosely

adverb

— moroseness

noun [noncount]

mundane
/ˌmʌnˈdeɪn/
adjective
[more mundane; most mundane]
1
: dull and ordinary

2
: relating to ordinary life on earth rather than to spiritual things

¹ nettle

/ˈnɛtl̩/

verb

nettles; **nettled**; **nettling**

[+ object]

: to make (someone) angry

² nettle

/ˈnɛtl̩/

noun

plural **nettles**

[count]

: a tall plant that has leaves with hairs that sting you if you touch them

grasp the nettle

British

: to deal with an unpleasant situation without delay

obdurate

/ˈɑːbdərət/ Brit /ˈɒbdjərət/

adjective

[more obdurate; most obdurate] *formal*

: refusing to do what other people want : not willing to change your opinion or the way you do something : STUBBORN

— obduracy

/ˈɑːbdərəsi/ Brit /ˈɒbdjərəsi/ ***noun*** [noncount]

— obdurately

adverb

obtain
/əbˈteɪn/
verb
obtains; obtained; obtaining
1
[+ object] *somewhat formal* : to gain or get (something) usually by effort

2
not used in progressive tenses, [no object] *formal* : to continue to be accepted or in use

— obtainable

/əbˈteɪnəbəl/ *adjective*, *formal*

obviate
/ˈɑːbviˌeɪt/
verb
obviates; obviated; obviating
[+ object] *formal*
: to make (something) no longer necessary

: to prevent or avoid (something)

[1] jibe

/ˈdʒaɪb/

verb

jibes; jibed; jibing

[no object] *US, informal*

: to agree *with* someone or something

[2] jibe

/ˈdʒaɪb/

verb

jibes; jibed; jibing

[no object]

: to cause a sailboat to change direction by swinging the sail to the opposite side of the boat

oppress

/əˈprɛs/

verb

oppresses; oppressed; oppressing

[+ object]

1

: to treat (a person or group of people) in a cruel or unfair way

2

: to make (someone) feel sad or worried for a long period of time — usually used as *(be) oppressed*

the oppressed

: people who are oppressed

— oppression

/əˈprɛʃən/ ***noun*** [noncount]

irresolute
/ɪˈrɛsəˌluːt/
adjective
[more irresolute; most irresolute] *formal*
: not certain about what to do : not resolute

— irresolutely

adverb
irksome
/ˈɚksəm/
adjective
[more irksome; most irksome]
: annoying or irritating

interpret
/ɪnˈtɚprət/
verb
interprets; interpreted; interpreting
1
[+ object] : to explain the meaning of (something)

2
[+ object] : to understand (something) in a specified way

— often + *as*

3
[+ object] : to perform (something, such as a song or a role) in a way that shows your own thoughts and feelings about it

4

[no object] : to translate the words that someone is speaking into a different language : to repeat what someone says in a different language than the language originally used

— interpretable

/ɪnˈtɚprətəbəl/ *adjective* [more interpretable; most interpretable]

inscrutable
/ɪnˈskru:təbəl/
adjective
[more inscrutable; most inscrutable] *formal*
: difficult to understand : causing people to feel curious or confused

— inscrutability

/ɪnˌskru:təˈbɪləti/ *noun* [noncount]

— inscrutably

/ɪnˈskru:təbli/ *adverb*

ingratiate
/ɪnˈgreɪʃiˌeɪt/
verb
ingratiates; ingratiated; ingratiating
[+ object] *often disapproving*
: to gain favor or approval for (yourself) by doing or saying things that people like — usually + *with*

indefatigable
/ˌɪndɪˈfætɪɡəbəl/
adjective
[more indefatigable; most indefatigable] *formal*
: able to work or continue for a very long time without becoming tired : TIRELESS

— indefatigably

/ˌɪndɪˈfætɪɡəbli/ *adverb*

[1] **incidental**
/ˌɪnsəˈdɛntl̟/
adjective
[more incidental; most incidental]
: happening as a minor part or result of something else
— often + *to*

[2] **incidental**
/ˌɪnsəˈdɛntl̟/
noun
plural **incidentals**
[count]
: something that happens as a minor part or result of something else : something
that is incidental — usually plural

implacable
/ɪmˈplækəbəl/
adjective
[more implacable; most implacable]
: opposed to someone or something in a very angry or determined way that cannot
be changed

— implacably

/ɪmˈplækəbli/ *adverb*

ignominy
/ˈɪgnəˌmɪni/
noun
plural **ignominies**
formal
: a situation or event that causes you to feel ashamed or embarrassed
[noncount][count]

ignominious
/ˌɪgnəˈmɪnijəs/
adjective
[more ignominious; most ignominious] *formal*
: causing disgrace or shame

— ignominiously

adverb

hypothesis
/ˌhaɪˈpɑːθəsəs/
noun
plural **hypotheses** /-əˌsiːz/ /ˌhaɪˈpɑːθəˌsiːz/
[count]
: an idea or theory that is not proven but that leads to further study or discussion

scrutinize
verb
or British **scrutinise** /ˈskruːtəˌnaɪz/
scrutinizes; scrutinized; scrutinizing
[+ object]
: to examine (something) carefully especially in a critical way

widespread
/ˈwaɪdˈsprɛd/
adjective
[more widespread; most widespread]
: common over a wide area or among many people

waive
/ˈweɪv/
verb
waives; waived; waiving
[+ object]
: to officially say that you will not use or require something that you are allowed to have or that is usually required

vilify
/ˈvɪləˌfaɪ/
verb
vilifies; vilified; vilifying
[+ object] *formal*
: to say or write very harsh and critical things about (someone or something)

— vilification

/ˌvɪləfəˈkeɪʃən/ ***noun*** [noncount]

vestige
/ˈvɛstɪdʒ/
noun
plural **vestiges**
[count] *formal*
1
: the last small part that remains of something that existed before : <u>TRACE</u> — + *of*

2
: the smallest possible amount of something — + *of* — usually used in negative statements

turgid
/ˈtə·dʒəd/
adjective
[more turgid; most turgid] *formal*
1
disapproving : very complicated and difficult to understand

2
: larger or fuller than normal because of swelling

sustain
/səˈsteɪn/
verb
sustains; sustained; sustaining
[+ object]
1
: to provide what is needed for (something or someone) to exist, continue, etc.

2
formal : to hold up the weight of (something)

3
formal : to deal with or experience (something bad or unpleasant) : <u>SUFFER</u>

4
law : to decide or state that (something) is proper, legal, or fair

5
formal : to show that (something) is true or correct : to confirm or prove (something)

stupendous
/stʊˈpɛndəs/ Brit /stjʊˈpɛndəs/
adjective
[more stupendous; most stupendous]
: so large or great that it amazes you

— **stupendously**

Adverb

[1] **stable**
/ˈsteɪbəl/
adjective
stabler; stablest
[also more stable; most stable]
1
a : in a good state or condition that is not easily changed or likely to change

b *medical* : not getting worse or likely to get worse

2
: not easily moved

3

: emotionally or mentally healthy : calm and reasonable

4

technical : having a chemical structure or physical state that does not change easily

² stable
/ˈsteɪbəl/
noun
plural **stables**
[count]
1
: a building in which horses are kept, fed, and cared for

— sometimes used in the plural form **stables** especially to mean a place where horses are kept for riding lessons

2
a : the group of racehorses that belong to the same owner

b : a group of people (such as athletes, writers, or performers) who work for or are trained by the same person, organization, or business

c : a group of products that are made by the same company

³ stable
/ˈsteɪbəl/
verb
stables; stabled; stabling
[+ object]
: to put or keep (a horse) in a stable

simper
/ˈsɪmpɚ/
verb
simpers; simpered; simpering
1
[no object] : to smile in a way that is not sincere or natural

2
[+ object] : to say (something) in a way that is not sincere or natural

— **simper**

noun [singular]

— **simpering**

adjective

glib
/ˈglɪb/
adjective
glibber; glibbest
[also more glib; most glib] *disapproving*
1
: said or done too easily or carelessly : showing little preparation or thought

2
: speaking in a smooth, easy way that is not sincere

— **glibly**

adverb

— **glibness**

noun [noncount]

retrieve
/rɪˈtriːv/
verb
retrieves; retrieved; retrieving
1
[+ object]
a : to get and bring (something) back from a place

b : to find and get (information) from a computer or disk

2
: to find and bring birds or animals that have been shot back to a hunter
[no object]

[+ object]

3
[+ object] *formal* : to keep (something) from failing or becoming worse

— **retrievable**

/rɪˈtriːvəbəl/ *adjective*

renegade
/ˈrɛnɪˌgeɪd/
noun
plural **renegades**
[count]
1
: a person who leaves one group, religion, etc., and joins another that opposes it

— usually used before another noun

2
: someone or something that causes trouble and cannot be controlled

— often used before another noun

redolent
/ˈrɛdələnt/
adjective
[more redolent; most redolent] *literary + formal*
1
: having a strong smell : full of a fragrance or odor

— often + *of*

— often + *with*

2
: causing thoughts or memories *of* something

rebuke
/rɪˈbjuːk/
verb
rebukes; **rebuked**; **rebuking**
[+ object] *formal*
: to speak in an angry and critical way to (someone) — often + *for*

— **rebuke**

noun, plural **rebukes** [count]

¹ range
/ˈreɪndʒ/
noun
plural **ranges**
1
[count] : a group or collection of different things or people that are usually similar
in some way — usually singular — usually + *of*

2
[count] : a series of numbers that includes the highest and lowest possible
amounts — usually singular

3

[count] : the total amount of ability, knowledge, experience, etc., that a person has — usually singular

4

[count] : all of the notes that a particular person can sing or that a particular musical instrument can make — usually singular

querulous
/ˈkweɚ-jələs/
adjective
[more querulous; most querulous] *formal*
: complaining in an annoyed way

— **querulously**

adverb

— **querulousness**

noun [noncount]

proximity
/prɑkˈsɪməti/
noun
[noncount]
: the state of being near

— often + *to*

[1] **prior**

/ˈprajɚ/

adjective

always used before a noun

1

: existing earlier in time : PREVIOUS

2

formal : more important than something else because it came first

prior to

somewhat formal

: before (a time, event, etc.)

[2] **prior**

/ˈprajɚ/

noun

plural **priors**

[count]

1

a : a monk who is the head of a religious house or order

b : a priest whose rank is just below that of an abbot

2

US, informal : a previous time of being arrested for or found guilty of a crime

platitude

/ˈplætəˌtuːd/ Brit /ˈplætəˌtjuːd/

noun

plural **platitudes**

[count] *disapproving*

: a statement that expresses an idea that is not new

— platitudinous

/ˌplætəˈtuːdnəs/ Brit /ˌplætəˈtjuːdnəs/ *adjective, formal* [more platitudinous; most platitudinous]

permeate
/ˈpɚmiˌeɪt/
verb
permeates; permeated; permeating
formal
: to pass or spread through (something)
[+ object][no object]

peremptory
/pəˈrɛmptəri/
adjective
[more peremptory; most peremptory] *formal*
1
— used to describe an order, command, etc., that you must obey without any questions or excuses

2
disapproving : having or showing the insulting attitude of people who think that they should be obeyed without question : ARROGANT

— peremptorily

/pəˈrɛmptərəli/ *adv*

bestow
/bɪˈstoʊ/
verb
bestows; **bestowed**; **bestowing**
[+ object] *formal*
: to give (something) as a gift or honor

credence
/ˈkriːdn̩s/
noun
[noncount]
1
: belief that something is true

2
: the quality of being believed or accepted as something true or real

corpulent
/ˈkoɚpjələnt/
adjective
[more corpulent; most corpulent] *formal*
: fat

— corpulence

/ˈkoɚpjələns/ ***noun*** [noncount]

copious
/ˈkoʊpijəs/
adjective
always used before a noun
: very large in amount or number

— **copiously**

adverb

construe
/kənˈstruː/
verb
construes; construed; construing
[+ object] *somewhat formal*
1
: to understand (an action, event, remark, etc.) in a particular way — usually + *as*

— often used as *(be) construed*

— compare MISCONSTRUE
2
: to understand the meaning of (a word, phrase, or sentence)

cogent
/ˈkoʊʤənt/
adjective
[more cogent; most cogent] *formal*
: very clear and easy for the mind to accept and believe

— **cogency**

/ˈkoʊʤənsi/ ***noun*** [noncount]

— **cogently**

adverb

coalesce
/ˌkowəˈlɛs/
verb
coalesces; coalesced; coalescing
[no object] *formal*
: to come together to form one group or mass

— **coalescence**

/ˌkowəˈlɛsn̩s/ ***noun***
[noncount]

[singular]

circumspect
/ˈsɚkəmˌspɛkt/
adjective
[more circumspect; most circumspect] *formal*
: thinking carefully about possible risks before doing or saying something

— **circumspection**

/ˌsɚkəmˈspɛkʃən/ ***noun*** [noncount]

— **circumspectly**

/ˈsɚkəmˌspɛktli/ ***adverb***

candid
/ˈkændəd/
adjective
[more candid; most candid]
1
: expressing opinions and feelings in an honest and sincere way

2
photography : showing people acting in a natural way because they do not know that they are being photographed

— **candidly**

adverb

— **candidness**

noun [noncount]

callous
/ˈkæləs/
adjective
[more callous; most callous] *disapproving*
: not feeling or showing any concern about the problems or suffering of other people

— **callously**

adverb

— **callousness**

noun [noncount]

bulwark
/ˈbʊlˌwɚk/
noun
plural **bulwarks**
[count]
1
formal : something that provides protection for or against something

2
: a wall that is built for protection : <u>RAMPART</u>
3
: a wall that is part of a ship's sides and that is above the ship's upper deck —
  usually plural

bucolic
/bjuˈkɑːlɪk/
adjective
literary + formal
: of or relating to the country or country life : <u>PASTORAL</u>

bland
/ˈblænd/
adjective
blander; blandest
1
: not interesting or exciting

2
: lacking strong flavor

3
: showing no emotion, concern, etc.

— **blandly**

adverb

— **blandness**

noun [noncount]

credible
/ˈkrɛdəbəl/
adjective
[more credible; most credible]
1
: able to be believed : reasonable to trust or believe

2
: good enough to be effective

— **credibly**

/ˈkrɛdəbli/ *adverb*

belie
/bɪˈlaɪ/
verb
belies; belied; belying
[+ object] *formal*
1
: to give a false idea of (something)
2
: to show (something) to be false or wrong

banter
/ˈbæntɚ/
noun
[noncount]
: talk in which people make jokes about each other in a friendly way

— **banter**

verb **banters; bantered; bantering** [no object]

bane
/ˈbeɪn/
noun
[singular]
: a cause of trouble, annoyance, or unhappiness — usually used in the phrase **the bane of**

avarice
/ˈævərəs/
noun
[noncount] *formal* + *disapproving*
: a strong desire to have or get money : <u>GREED</u>

— avaricious

/ˌævəˈrɪʃəs/ *adjective* [more avaricious; most avaricious]

augment
/ɑgˈmɛnt/
verb
augments; augmented; augmenting
[+ object] *formal*
1
: to increase the size or amount of (something)

— often used as *(be) augmented*

2
US : to add something to (something) in order to improve or complete it

— augmentation

/ˌɑːgmənˈteɪʃən/ *noun* [noncount]

askance
/əˈskæns/
adverb
: in a way that shows a lack of trust or approval

arbitrary
/ˈɑɚbəˌtreri/ Brit /ˈɑːbətrəri/
adjective
1
[more arbitrary; most arbitrary] : not planned or chosen for a particular reason

: not based on reason or evidence

2
: done without concern for what is fair or right

— **arbitrarily**

/ˌɑɚbəˈtrerəli/ Brit /ˈɑːbətrərəli/ ***adverb***

— **arbitrariness**

/ˈɑɚbəˌtrerinəs/ Brit /ˈɑːbətrərinəs/ ***noun*** [noncount]

ambiguous
/æmˈbɪgjəwəs/
adjective
[more ambiguous; most ambiguous]
1
: able to be understood in more than one way : having more than one possible meaning

— opposite <u>UNAMBIGUOUS</u>

Synonyms see: [1]OBSCURE

2

: not expressed or understood clearly

— **ambiguously**

adverb

alacrity

/əˈlækrəti/

noun

: a quick and cheerful readiness to do something

[noncount]

[singular]

[1] **accord**

/əˈkoɚd/

noun

plural **accords**

1

[count] : a formal or official agreement

2

[noncount] : a situation or state in which people or things agree

of its own accord

◊ If something happens *of its own accord*, it happens by itself without anyone causing it to happen.

of your own accord

◊ If you do something *of your own accord*, you do it because you want to, not because someone has asked you or forced you to do it.

with one accord

chiefly British, formal
: all together

² accord
/əˈkoɚd/
verb
accords; accorded; according
[+ object] *formal*
: to give (something, such as special treatment or status) to someone or something

accord with

[phrasal verb]
accord with (something)
: to be in agreement with (something)

ensue
/ɪnˈsuː/ Brit /ɪnˈsjuː/
verb
ensues; ensued; ensuing
[no object]
: to come at a later time : to happen as a result

— ensuing

adjective

gibe
noun
or **jibe** /ˈdʒaɪb/
plural **gibes** *or* **jibes**
[count]
: an insulting or critical remark that is meant to hurt someone or make someone appear foolish

generate
/ˈdʒɛnəˌreɪt/
verb
generates; **generated**; **generating**
[+ object]
1
: to produce (something) or cause (something) to be produced

2
: to be the cause of or reason for (something, such as interest or excitement)

— **generative**

/ˈdʒɛnrətɪv/ ***adjective***, *technical*

frustrate
/ˈfrʌˌstreɪt/
verb
frustrates; **frustrated**; **frustrating**
[+ object]
1
: to cause (someone) to feel angry, discouraged, or upset because of not being able to do something
2
: to prevent (efforts, plans, etc.) from succeeding
: to keep (someone) from doing something

fluctuate
/ˈflʌktʃəˌweɪt/
verb
fluctuates; fluctuated; fluctuating
[no object]
: to change level, strength, or value frequently

— fluctuation

/ˌflʌktʃəˈweɪʃən/ ***noun****, plural* **fluctuations**
[count][noncount]

fiasco
/fiˈæskoʊ/
noun
plural **fiascoes**
[count]
: a complete failure or disaster

feasible
/ˈfiːzəbəl/
adjective
[more feasible; most feasible]
: possible to do
/ˌfiːzəˈbɪləti/ ***noun*** [noncount]

— feasibly

/ˈfiːzəbli/ ***adverb***

fatuous
/ˈfætʃuwəs/
adjective
[more fatuous; most fatuous]
: foolish or stupid

— **fatuously**

adverb

— **fatuousness**

noun [noncount]

exploit
/ˈɛkˌsploɪt/
noun
plural **exploits**
[count]
: an exciting act or action — usually plural

[2] **exploit**
/ɪkˈsploɪt/
verb
exploits; exploited; exploiting
[+ object]
1
: to get value or use from (something)
2
: to use (someone or something) in a way that helps you unfairly

— exploitable

/ɪkˈsplɔɪtəbəl/ *adjective* [more exploitable; most exploitable]

— exploitation

/ˌɛkˌsplɔɪˈteɪʃən/ *noun* [noncount]

— exploiter

noun, *plural* **exploiters** [count]

expatiate
/ɛkˈspeɪʃiˌeɪt/
verb
expatiates; expatiated; expatiating
[no object] *formal*
: to speak or write about something in a way that includes a lot of details or uses many words — usually + *on* or *upon*

evaluate
/ɪˈvæljəˌweɪt/
verb
evaluates; evaluated; evaluating
[+ object]
: to judge the value or condition of (someone or something) in a careful and thoughtful way

— evaluation

/ɪˌvæljəˈweɪʃən/ *noun*, *plural* **evaluations**
[count][noncount]

— evaluative

/ɪˈvæljəˌweɪtɪv/ Brit /ɪˈvæljuətɪv/ *adjective, formal*

— evaluator

/ɪˈvæljəˌweɪtɚ/ *noun, plural* **evaluators** [count]

[1] **estimate**
/ˈɛstəmət/
noun
plural **estimates**
1
[count] : a guess that you make based on the information you have about the size, amount, etc., of something
2
[count] : a statement about how much a job will cost
3
: an opinion or judgment about how good or bad something is
[singular][noncount]

[2] **estimate**
/ˈɛstəˌmeɪt/
verb
estimates; estimated; estimating
[+ object]
: to give or form a general idea about the value, size, or cost of (something) : to make an estimate of (something)

— estimated

adjective

— estimator

/ˈɛstəˌmeɪtɚ/ **noun**, *plural* **estimators** [count]

entreat
/ɪnˈtriːt/
verb
entreats; entreated; entreating
[+ object] *formal*
: to ask (someone) in a serious and emotional way
accede
/ækˈsiːd/
verb
accedes; acceded; acceding
[no object] *formal*
1
: to agree to a request or a demand — usually + *to*

2
: to enter a high office or position

— usually + *to*

effete
/ɪˈfiːt/
adjective
[more effete; most effete] *disapproving*
1
: lacking strength, courage, or spirit

2
: resembling a woman : EFFEMINATE

edict
/'iː dɪkt/
noun
plural **edicts**
[count]
: an official order given by a person with power or by a government : DECREE

divulge
/də'vʌldʒ/
verb
divulges; **divulged**; **divulging**
[+ object] *formal*
: to make (information) known : to give (information) to someone

distribute
/dɪ'strɪbjuːt/
verb
distributes; **distributed**; **distributing**
[+ object]
1
a : to give or deliver (something) to people

— usually + *to*

b : to deliver (something) to a store or business — usually + *to*

2
: to divide (something) among the members of a group — usually
+ *between* or *among* — often used as *(be/get) distributed*

3
: to spread or place (something) over an area

— often used as *(be/get) distributed*

— often used figuratively

discursive
/dɪˈskɚsɪv/
adjective
[more discursive; most discursive] *formal*
: talking or writing about many different things in a way that is not highly organized

— **discursively**

adverb

disconcert
/ˌdɪskənˈsɚt/
verb
disconcerts; disconcerted; disconcerting
[+ object] *somewhat formal*
: to make (someone) upset or embarrassed

— often used as *(be) disconcerted*

— **disconcerted**

/ˌdɪskənˈsɚtəd/ ***adjective*** [more disconcerted; most disconcerted]

— **disconcerting**

/ˌdɪskənˈsɚtɪŋ/ ***adjective*** [more disconcerting; most disconcerting]

— disconcertingly

adverb

diffident
/ˈdɪfɪdənt/
adjective
[more diffident; most diffident]
1
: lacking confidence : not feeling comfortable around people

2
: very careful about acting or speaking

— diffidence

/ˈdɪfədəns/ ***noun*** [noncount]

— diffidently

adverb

didactic
/daɪˈdæktɪk/
adjective
[more didactic; most didactic] *formal*
1
: designed or intended to teach people something

2
usually disapproving — used to describe someone or something that tries to teach something (such as proper or moral behavior) in a way that is annoying or unwanted

— didactically

/daɪˈdæktɪkli/ *adverb*

deplete

/dɪˈpliːt/
verb
depletes; depleted; depleting
[+ object]
: to use most or all of (something important) : to greatly reduce the amount of (something)— often used as *(be) depleted*

— depletion

/dɪˈpliːʃən/ *noun, plural* **depletions**
[count][noncount]

deference

/ˈdɛfərəns/
noun
[noncount] *formal*
: a way of behaving that shows respect for someone or something

— often + *to*

in deference to

or **out of deference to**
: in order to show respect for the opinions or influence of (someone or something) : out of respect for (someone or something)

— deferential

/ˌdɛfəˈrɛnʃəl/ *adjective* [more deferential; most deferential]

— deferentially

adverb

zealot

/ˈzɛlət/
noun
plural **zealots**
[count] *often disapproving*
: a person who has very strong feelings about something (such as religion or politics) and who wants other people to have those feelings : a zealous person

— zealotry

/ˈzɛlətri/ *noun* [noncount]

zenith

/ˈziːnəθ/ Brit /ˈzɛnəθ/
noun
[singular]
1
formal : the strongest or most successful period of time

— opposite <u>NADIR</u>
2
technical : the highest point reached in the sky by the sun, moon, etc.

References

1-Pyle, M. A. (2001). *TOEFL CBT*. IDG Books Worldwide.

2-Dictionary, M. W. (2002). Merriam-webster. *On-line at http://www. mw. com/home. htm*, *8*(2).

3-Gear, J., & Gear, R. (2002). *Cambridge Preparation for the TOEFL® Test Book with CD-ROM* (Vol. 1). Cambridge University Press.

4-Widiastuty, H., Qamariah, Z., & Mirza, A. A. (2020). *TOEFL VOCABULARY BUILDING*. Airlangga University Press.